FLIGHT MODE

FLIGHT MODE

JEN WEBB
SHÉ HAWKE

Flight Mode
Recent Work Press
Canberra, Australia

Copyright © Jen Webb and Shé Hawke, 2020

ISBN: 9780648936749 (paperback)

 A catalogue record for this book is available from the National Library of Australia

All rights reserved. This book is copyright. Except for private study, research, criticism or reviews as permitted under the Copyright Act, no part of this book may be reproduced, stored in a retrieval system, or transmitted in any form by any means without prior written permission. Enquiries should be addressed to the publisher.

Cover image: Travis Swicegood, 2015. Reproduced under Creative Commons Licence 2.0
Cover design: Recent Work Press
Set by Recent Work Press

recentworkpress.com

SS

Contents

PART 1: JEN WEBB

The possibilities of water	3
The language of fish	4
Lost and found	5
Unspeakable fragments	6
Afterwards	7
Asylum	8
When the music stops	9
The hangman	10
Fishing with Rex	11
On the banks of the Swan	12
In Crawley	13
The night watchman	14
Mt Gibson, 29.724°S, 117.1705°E	15
At the sandalwooders camp	16
Big cat tales	17
On not reading Proust	18
En route	20
Attunga Point, Lake Burley Griffin	21
The language of light	22
No objective correlative	23
Chicago, after the collapse	24
Mirrorskin	25
After Ovid	26
Icarus Icara	27
Births, deaths and marriages	28
Changing sides	30
Timing	31
Cape of storms	32
A line to god	33
Plain of jars	34
Icarus	35
Play it as it lays	37
Flight mode (for SH)	38

PART 2: SHÉ HAWKE

Mariana trench	43
Disturbing the peace	44
In the paper tonight	45
Mytho/Political waters	47
Un-Guard	49
Mont Blanc ice	51
Winded	52
Smalls (Haiku)	53
Micro Socialism	54
Gleaning	55
Refugee Mary	56
Threshold	58
Border-zones	59
Negev time	60
Airs	61
Yes Dante	62
Ode to Habitus	63
Slovenian Poems	65
Filtering	66
Skin	67
Fire	68
Fish	69
Brief-cased girl	70
Who am I?	71
The 7th Wave	72
Threes	73
The breath of trees	74
Friday night in Freo (circa 1985)	75
Disciple	76
Pre-Iconic capital	78
Lamentacious	80
I. Repose in the key of G	81
II. Repose in the key of B	82
III. Repose in a major key	83
IV. Repose as a major 7th	84
PS	85
Afterword	86

PART 1

JEN WEBB

The possibilities of water

I.

The sun falls too fast, denying its own vertigo, and the fisher folk pause between their boats and the sea to watch it fall. The old man nods, knowing it all already, and you catch me up, saying *never mind*, knowing that this is just another smudge on the horizon of our story.

II.

When the sea scolds the rocks, when the sea caresses the rocks, you stand on the great grey rocks and hold your nerve no matter the angle of the waves. The water reaches for you, reminds you that this is home. Take your chances. Expect no grace. It's you, and unending love, and the inquisitive sea.

III.

So lower the sounding line. Feed it fathom by fathom into the water. Each knot calls its mark as it passes the palm of your hand. Deeper and deeper, the lead seeks out the depths, swaying. We are taking soundings, we are calling the deep. We will not run aground.

The language of fish

The Guinness is dark and deep. I have been swimming for years, surfacing occasionally to catch up on news, to find out how the world is turning. Then it's back down, into the dark. It's lonely here, but I'm not alone: small fish live nearby, and on heartbreak nights I eavesdrop on their conversations, listen to the grunts and chirps that pass with them for speech. The Guinness is more effective: I breathe it in, remembering drinks and lovers now long gone. I try to tell the fish about it, but their syntax is beyond me.

Lost and found

I.

You sweep up the crumbs and throw them on the lawn. Tomorrow you will make soup and put the scraps in the bin. Tomorrow you will not make that call. The wind is full of promise, though it famously never makes good. We speak of it in shadows, our phrases full of blame. Still, we are quite easily satisfied. You say *soup* and I pass you a bowl. You say *sorrow* and I hand you the phone.

II.

It's been raining nonstop and that plus the hail has wrecked our garden and shredded our nerves. Time is not on our side: we have been coming and going, heating and drying, forgetting our delights, forgetting how to retune the set. The rain is filling the world. Is this where it all comes to rest? Our house has braced its back, the garden soil has opened tiny mouths, and the word 'slaked' whispers through recordings I made while checking up on you. I am slaked, I am satiated, you are packing up and leaving, it can't come soon enough.

Unspeakable fragments

I.

My hands, all over your skin. You taste of brine and cold seaweed. I lift your hand and kiss it. Place it on my breast, between my thighs. Now your blank eye observes me, blankly. The things we planned. The things we did not do. It was not supposed to be like this. I lift your hand, lick away the brine, taste my skin on you, taste my cunt. Walk away.

II.

He must have blundered awkwardly into the web, which was wrapped around him like a ... one person said lover, one said shawl. He should have taken a different route. He should never have. Surely there'd be a way out? We looked. We clustered beneath the web, staring up at where he hung, where he had ceased to struggle. Someone began to say. Someone coughed. The web was damaged, but still it held him. Like ... a mother? Like chains? Someone poked him gently, but he failed to respond. The web swayed. Small unspeakable fragments shivered loose and fell among us, and we leapt back, brushing at our own shoulders, pushing each other aside. We hammered a warning sign at the start of the path. We told his wife that he had gone.

Afterwards

The storm broke overhead, and in seconds Mort Street was waist deep. Three men were washed away in the wake of buses passing while I watched, with strangers, under the 7-11 storefront.

It stopped as quickly as it started, and I was only eight minutes late when I joined you at our favourite table in Iori. The waiter brought smoky tea and you held me like I was the one that got away, till I fishtailed out of your arms and took up the menu.

Outside it stormed again, and the waters rose, and I was hungry for more than you. Calmly, I ordered agedashi.

Asylum

He moved in with us one summer; huddled
fevered on the deck, his feathers awry.
We caught him, at last, clipped the thread
from his leg, and when he healed
he left for home.

Each year they come, and keep coming, these
damaged birds. You lose a few, but still
we set out seed and keep the birdbath fresh.
They land at dusk, gather below the tree;
exchange their tales.

We fished him from the watertank, dull eyed,
almost dead. Dried his feathers; put him in a cage.
It took weeks till he was well. He peered out,
watchfully, took a step, then spread his new wings.
They keep coming, passing through. This is no

parliament of fowls; no divisions called, no
laws proposed. The raptors circle overhead
waiting for a moment's inattention, but
we patrol the yard. We have learned their ways.
We freshen the water, keep the cats in check.

When the music stops

Everything stops. She puts her pen on the desk, she puts her notebook on the desk. Words are out there, circling. They approach her when she stretches out her hand palm up, but they won't land.

She still bears the scars of the last time a word hooked its talons in her thumb. Remembering that now, remembering the ache, she lifts her hand to her mouth and kisses it better.

Any kiss will do, in a pinch. Any storm will do, when you are in its eye.

The music starts, and coughs, and jumps track to a piece she'd forgotten, where German horses thunder and Nordic Christs bleed through the strings. None of this is safe; none of this will work. Get out of the house, fast.

The hangman

White hands. White masks. You are far below the surface where lines break at unlikely junctions and all is refraction, all confound. There's the smell of what must be teeth, burning. Salt in your eyes. There's a man too close, asking questions you can't fathom. He is making the shapes of sounds – his mouth opens and closes silently, a fish out of water. Is it *oh,* you ask him; is it *ell?* He makes the sign of the hangman and turns, slowly, his back toward you.

Fishing with Rex

In autumn you took me fishing. We stood at the ocean's edge, casting lines across the waves. You taught me to thread worms on hooks, pierce them below the head, above the gut—a small murder. I loved the whirr of line through reel, the quick turn of wrist, a sinker flying its weight out to sea, the creel against my hip, standing still while waves blustered about our legs, grey water sluicing pitted rocks.

Wet to the waist we cast and reeled; I learned the weight of line and rod, the weight of fish: modest steenbras; a galjoen or two; sometimes a snoek; you pointed out a fin's flicker, the silver thread, how shadows flow; you propped your bamboo rod against your belt, I held my little rod, and watched ships sail around the point and off horizon's edge.

You kept few fish—too small, you said, too young, you held their bodies, wrestled hooks from mouths in suffocating air: the weather rolling in; tourists gathering towels, running for cars. I feared nothing; steadied against the tide I leaned against you, listening to gulls call in a minor key, to percussive waves and a child's pitched cry, till the sun set beside us, and we carried the rods home, carrying the creel, watching the air flicker red and silver, fearing nothing; every breath an orison, every flutter of light a note of grace.

On the banks of the Swan

The river is dreaming tonight. Christmas lights drift below the cupped palm of its surface; busy ferries colour between lines that only they can see.

It is nearly year end. The dead are dreaming tonight, imagining themselves back with those they loved. They taste again the salt of a lover's skin. They ache to nurse the newborn child.

They knock at the door, rattle the locks, but only fellow dead turn to see who's there. As December becomes January, and the living fox the pages of the new year, they lose heart, cease to call.

In Crawley

Ducks bellyflopping in the Chancellor's private pool. Deep cloisters racketed by beatboxing boys. The groundsmen watch them darkly from behind mouthsful of smoke beside the no smoking sign while in the Chinese garden the fake cascade coughs itself into a cloudy pond ghosted by koi that move slowly below the high-backed bridge, a gesture of golden fin, a shadow on the surface. Hiphop clatters between bamboo stalks thick as your arm. The sun sets across the Indian Ocean but the light doesn't fade.

The night watchman

A lyrebird that can
sing like Te Kanawa but
makes the sound
of a chainsaw.

Cats exchanging purrs for yowls.

The chickens shriek in the night
starting us from our bed. Foxes
I guess, or bad dreams. You ran naked

across wet grass and sharp
gravel to check the locks
to soothe the hens.

Skies crammed with inquisitive stars. The aging
gum tree groaned and shifted its feet.

For weeks after
my dreams were
of foxes, and of tearing, and of
the end of things.

Mt Gibson, 29.724°S, 117.1705°E

I.

What we did was dive right in: walk into a moonscape and set up camp, you and me and the kids, and a dog we picked up on the way. This is our chance, you said. The children scattered, warping up the trees; the dog stayed close. We might have made it, but for summer. Wild dogs came, and nothing survived: not the lambs or the joey or the hens. We scooped up their bodies and buried them where they fell, set up cairns to confound the ghosts.

II.

The only place the voices fell quiet was by the chook run where he set up the saw and sliced dead trees into wood. Headphones muting the orchestra of wind in wire fences, of hens singing or sheep calling out to each other, the distant nazgul cry of cockatoos. Haul cut stack. And repeat. Muscles bruised, woodpile growing. If he can maintain the pace, his voices will be calm, and the family survive another day.

III.

Your bike careens toward the highway, the back wheel slip-sliding, and your heart slides too, and you ride on. There's the high thin voice of your watch calling out the countdown, there's bugs in your hair, there's a sword suspended over the abyss. If you make it before the deadline. Your fractious heart, the sharp edges of wind in your eyes. The minute hand slows down, stretching out time, and if that doesn't fix this mess, then nothing will.

IV.

The children left, one by one, and then you left too, heading deeper into desert. Last I saw you were treading water across dry lake, and then you vanished into mirage and it was just me, and the sorrowful dog, and the red sand, shimmering.

At the sandalwooders camp

When the sandalwooders arrived the dogs went crazy, hating them: men who came as strangers. Locals said they perform dark deeds. Locals keep their horses penned and dogs loose. 'Good dog', we said to ours, when they barked. 'Good dog'. At night I walked through the trees. Humpeys and tents disguised as hills, shadowed forms against the horizon, air thick with unburned oil. They sat around their fires, passing joints, passing bottles, spitting on the ground. Beyond the fireline their ancient trucks spat fuel across dry leaves. I watched, until it felt wrong, then crept back to the homestead, trailing their scent.

Big cat tales

It's dry country where we live. There's cougars there, the hunters said, and lion. Experts shook their heads, but the hunters laid their bait, waited in their hides. Yes the big cats came, they said, and paused like ghosts for photos that never came out. They came, the hunters said, and left spoor and scat that blew away.

I believed them, though the experts did not. I had watched from the ute as something calmly walked past. Something gold, with legs and black points. Yellow eyes; haunches narrow and low. Ever since, when the light moves in a certain way, I see the world move with it and I smell my own skin: feline, and rank.

On not reading Proust

I keep it on the table by my bed. Con

                vincing myself I'll read it some

     day. Or some day   impress

                        a lover   I need

        to impress.

              It's slighter

than I'd thought. Still

     every sentence crushes me

              how the Romans
              crushed

        the doomed – elephants tramp

        ling those they'd marked for death,

        how the French heaped stones on

        the damned

        til they died.
        (It took days. Historians say)

When I lift Proust's book

                        I feel its weight. I

                                            bite

        a madeline   and taste   only tannin.

En route

By the third day we'd found
our feet. Which corner
was the right road home, who
sold the better sandwich.

We moved easily between
foreign towers, saw our own
faces on their screens.

How good the wine after work, how
fine the day before the storm
broke, washing us together
rinsing us away.

Attunga Point, Lake Burley Griffin

They came down to the lake, hefting
theodolites and string, tracing
a path through skeins of grass
between sentinel trees to where
light skittered on water, to where birds
cried the hour. The past
was all breath here, dust and old bones,
tree roots like rock, and that old game
democracy and all its bright dreams,
were shadowed in depths.

The wake of a boat washes
the banks, flutters curtains
in the drowned shacks below, disturbs
the sleeping dust of the race course
below. You break out the picnic basket,
distribute cups. Streets arc across the lake,
trees rust in cooling air. We sit silent on
this half beach, listening to the city
as water trembles, tracing out old tales of huts
and sheep, of men who made laws, and plans
for when it might be no more hard scrabble
on hard-scrabble ground. Someone pours
the coffee. Between the mirror lake and
the mirrored sky you lift a cup, look up. The sun
returns your gaze.

The language of light

All love turns finally to lament, but don't fret, dearest. The sun will rise and set regardless. We have watched it rise over the Indian Ocean, over the Atlantic, the Pacific. We marked it with dawn champagne, affirmations of eternity. Speaking too soon. Later we saw it set over the Tasman Sea; the next year we watched it slip away behind Lake Moore. By the time we stood watching it stain the waters of the Gulf, I was ready to go to law.

It was good while it lasted. We still have the photos and the stories and the fading scars and the legal judgments and the broken minds and the sleepless nights that keep us present to each other, rising and falling, turning and returning, bruising and healing and done.

No objective correlative

Dark matters. Clouds that move at a dead run across the sky, trying to get ahead of the storm. Headlines that clutter up the living room. But hey, you can't fix history. We sat up all night, drinking red wine, reading black-letter law, but there was nothing we could use to put the world to right. The shame of it. Never mind: we sat up all night, drinking white wine, our bodies intertwined. The more I drank, the more poems I recalled. The more you drank, the more you smiled. We made it through to morning.

Chicago, after the collapse

The ice was yellow by the time we got there, but no one complained. At least we had arrived. At least spring had arrived, and was waiting there, something louche in its half-warm touch. Not one of us was mugged, though the tourist guides had warned and though we went out searching.

Every night, new American dreams.

On one street a man stopped us with menaces, then sang an old blues standard, and asked only for cigarettes and praise. At Kapoor's Bean a man took my camera, but gave it back after shooting us, once we gave him peppermints and gum.

The buildings looked like Chicago should. The bars and grills were as they had promised. And as they had promised I fell in love, not easily, but well. The lights in the night sky, the lights on the frozen river, the lights leading away from here.

Everything in the right place.

Mirrorskin

I.

The barista moves slowly; we are dull today; waiting; ageing as we wait; our cells breathe and die, skin sloughs; nature is checking the contract. The word I'm looking for is something like 'untenable': we have made nothing happen that would not anyway have happened. Never mind. Coffee arrives, finally, the whorl on the crema mirroring the curl of the foetus in your womb, which mirrors the tiny bones deep inside my skull, which are a perfect match for the patterns on the shell we found on the beach after last year's storm. My fingerprints are emblazoned on your skin, a pattern of the world.

II.

Your skin is not your skin: there is nothing you can do to persuade it to your way of thinking. It knows itself, and only itself. Or that, and the scent of dry grass in winter; or that, and the fine line of fingers gliding across it; or that, and the touch of linen in spring. I have forgotten the way you held me, the weight of that pendant between my breasts, the last gasp of a faulty shower in a cheap hotel. I have forgotten. Still, my skin recalls, and it turns those sensations over and over, impressing them into memory.

After Ovid

I.

The first time you came to me in urgent scatter of wing. The next time you were heavy shoulder, dark eye. I knew you still, by your weight, by your heat, by my ludicrous desire. I was young then, weighing no consequences; all I measured was desire. Now when you come for me, you come as gods do: in human beauty, bringing knowledge, bringing change.

II.

The sea draws back, draws air down to its diaphragm, holds that breath. We run to the waterline where sea anemones, exposed, gasp and writhe. You say there's always losers in every pack, and then turn your back on the sea. When it strikes, a person should bend, like grass in a storm. I duck and cover as the water descends, holding my breath, waiting for the change.

III.

You are; then you are not. Or rather, it is you become new. No more for you the body flowing through space. Now your movements are the pulse of sap beneath the skin. This is not the future you'd have chosen. What you need now is patience. You are become gesture: your flesh stiffened, your lovely feet splayed, your thighs the branching of trees. Take a last breath, burrow down below the surface. Perhaps there's a way through.

Icarus Icara

I.

How you fly, without engines or wings. It's the way dreams fly: in fragments. It's the way ash swirls in the sudden breeze. You are making good your escape, picturing a future of absolute quiet. There is no turning back, not now you've made your move.

II.

All promise and no gift. You scatter feathers across the surface of the sea and they lie like scars on its skin, troubling sailors the way clouds trouble the idea of sky, the way a butterfly's wings upset that idea you had, or thought you had. The one that was going to make it all better.

III.

The mountain deflates slowly, forgetting all its slow thoughts as it changes from rock to dust. In the landscape of its sigh, water finds its level, and now there are fresh cartographies: the gesture of hand against breast, the curve of a thigh. Once the sea has staked its claim, you can pitch a tent on the shore, and pretend that I am feather, you are wing.

Births, deaths and marriages

Our house

                                            built over a boneyard

on summer days   the ancient   dead

                                    exhale

      and shudder

                  the air is putrefaction.

You

              making things worse

building cemeteries

                                    on street corners

                  sending

      invitations   to the dead

damn fool, that's

                        no way to live.

                        We need a

                        better trick than that

        to fool Mr Death.

Changing sides

You brought me a green leaf—pandanus,
you said, pressing it into my hand. While your wife
looked on. Later: Asian coriander in a sprig,
pungent-dense, your wife watching.
I'm all the spice you'll ever need, she said.

Today, a branch from a curry plant:
to remember me, she said.

I breathe in its scent.

Timing

We had thought there was nothing there, til nothing became something. We had thought it a light thing, here today gone tomorrow, but it was not light, and tomorrow it was not gone. It grew more dense, as the bones and nerves and muscles we had overlooked began to shift beneath its skin. We shifted too, skin to skin, wrapping the something around us, keeping out the cold. Until the stillness in our corner of the room filled with human clatter that rushed toward us, then broke and flowed past, the wash of its passage tugging at our feet. We held each other above the flow, and if we moved at all, it was slowly. We held onto each other, and kept holding, until the barman called time. We could have made a break for it then, but our rhythm was wrong. Now, when we move, we will move apart, and the moving will be measured, and slow.

Cape of storms

Ships' bones trace the line of the coast, remnants
washed by the sea to pure form.

We watched it drown, one bad-storm night,
from the high pass above the Cape;

the storm punched the ship across the rocks and left it
there, its belly torn, howling as it died. Men in slickers

launched small craft and crept through walls of sea, picked
their way through rocks toward the lights. Arms gestured in a language

not of words—rescuers, braced against the banshee night, while
the ship foundered, and was gone, and the men were saved,

or not. For weeks they scraped the ocean for the dead. Waves
still shattered around the hull.

A line to god

He wakes at night. There's a sound he
can't resolve—something scratching at
the door? When he turns on the light
the sound fails. He reaches for a smoke,
opens the window, leans into the stars.

What you learn as a child remains in your
bones. He learned the holy book, read
stories in its crazy pages—how
God quizzed little Samuel every night,
how Job lost his consolations.

If he stares at a single star, it falls but
still it looks back: the word *numinous* comes
to mind, and he wonders what it means, drifts
into drifting thought, into memories of his small-
boy days when wishes worked each time,

when surely the lost toy would be found,
the monster soothed to sleep, when his father
would find his way back from the grave. Leave it.
There's no time like the present—he should sleep
but here it is, all ribbons and wrapping—

there's no time like the present, it's there
fresh each morning, he straps on his boots,
the water bottle clanks at his belt, the bush
path is waiting like the morning, the present,
and every new washed sky, waiting.

Plain of jars

It's not easy to get there; buses
will take you, small planes
land nearby. Stick to the paths.
Tourists pick their way between
the weeds, point their cameras at the jars. Jars? No one,

not even Lonely Planet
knows what they were for. Fermenting
wine, perhaps a room for lovers
perhaps a burial site. It smells like
old graveyards;
no one survived.

Someone is sketching the jars, someone is
setting a tripod, a guide gestures
at the sky. Lonely Planet promises
a gift store nearby, advises travellers
not to buy the fĕr.

At Stonehenge, years ago
when I stood on a leyline my bones
crackled, and for a moment my skin
glowed. In Hong Kong, a guide
showed me ossuaries
on the hills, told me
the stories they contain.

Each Sunday, on the road beyond our house,
that young woman is there at the roadside cross
putting fresh water in the jars, fresh flowers,
putting off her exhausted grief
she sits, a moment's stasis, while the cars pass.

Icarus

It starts with
a ... and the light
rises, and the
blood.

She wakes
each day with
a plan. Her boy bursts
from his bed, pins
on his wings
and tests the air.

Behind him, sour
as the day,
his father stares, burdened
thoughts and fears
there in
the halls of his
memory. See its
grammars fall.

Dead stars
become new worlds.
The last lost dignities of
his profession:
percept gives way
to concept, cor
relation is not
causation, his boy
tests the wings,
his wife shuts
the door, the
logic fails.

She draws
the blinds. *Don't go*—
the voice is very small
now he is falling, the
grammar
of flight fails
him and
he is fall
ing still

with each star that falls
a new world is made,
draw him back
into that
open field
so he will real
ise, so he can start
again.

Play it as it lays

Cars and bikes and scooters call out and the air rings with quartal chords, unresolved accidentals: ghost orchestras playing out of time. The restaurateur says: *A machine is less precise than a leaf.* Along the impure streets, trees stretch their backs, old women stretch their backs, a man rides his scooter through a building and off the kerb. The restaurateur says: *There's a very thin line between humidity and humility.* You look into every window, and see nothing you know, and now it's pissing down sound, quavers and semiquavers flooding the gutters, and you without an umbrella. You really don't belong here, do you?

Flight mode (for SH)

I.

'One day I will fall silent, for the love of humanity' (Nietzsche)

Somewhere between being and being done over: that's where we are. It is the silent zone where we neither send messages nor receive, neither live nor die. You have shut down all your devices but your skin will not be silenced. All across the skies, humans are moving to and fro, every nerve feeling out the absence, longing for touch. All across the skies, splinters of desire flutter down and wherever they land, clumps of anxiety grow. Turn off your flight mode, dearest. Speak in sounds I can hear, send me stories I can live by.

II.

'Once discovered, it was easy for you to find me; the difficulty henceforth will be to lose me' (Nietzsche)

I have polished my boots and painted my nails and poured on my leathers and straightened my hair, I have stretched out my muscles and goggled my eyes, I have waxed my feathers, I've said my goodbyes, I am testing the air, I am ready to fly.

III.

'If you look too long into the abyss, the abyss will look into you' (Nietzsche)

Pinned between this rock and that hard place I am crying uncle. If I escape, if I reach 30,000 feet, will you join me? You've heard that the universe howls at that altitude, that the wind will slap you till you shriek: you will not come. Come. I am pinned between your rock and my own hard place, and the abyss has looked too long into me. Come. If we hover there, below the flight paths of angels and way above the birds, we might become the light we need.

IV.

'In the end one experiences only oneself' (Nietzsche)

Trust me in this. I am more than angles in geometry, more than an axiom on someone else's pulse. I am an engine coughing up last night's cigars. When you find me I'll be downing the opiates you prescribed, I'll be reviewing my will. Sign here. Fold along the dotted line. The world is swarming under my feet, the trees are too steep, the rocks too sharp. I need to make a break. I need to find my wings.

V.
'When all is said and done, death' (Nietzsche)

She is almost too tired to reach for him. Fingertips will have to do: catch as catch can. He urges her to find her feet, to join the dance. Life only in movement, he says, and almost means it. She groans, but stretches her great black wings, and feels the muscles in her shoulders review the patterns of flight. Open the windows, switch off the lights. Now she's moving too fast, he can't keep up, he can't arrest her flight. He falls back to earth, watches the beat of the wings as she finds her rhythm, watches her slide out of his sight.

PART 2

SHÉ HAWKE

Mariana trench

If I could
I'd inject you like heroin
let you suck me
into your cavernous Hadean ditch
drag me useless
across the floor of your will
—rips and swells your emissaries—
rack, pound and swallow me
till I die a 1,000 little deaths
in your promise.

Disturbing the peace

When you disturb our peace
by waging war
on innocence,
you threaten the gentle
in us
yes, that's right, no 'I' statements here
—you threaten us
hold us hostage to your indifference

and we haven't even met

yet

you are everywhere present
both reckless and strategic
acting out
your infantile wounds
scarring the earth
with your fear,

trying to make it ours.

In the paper tonight

What we owe the innocent
those now endangered animals
—asphyxiating in the smoke of climate change—
is a trump card
to distill
the acid reflux
of fear and obsession,
to re-negotiate
a new global reference point
ethically cleansed from its own history
that has no need of a Trojan War
that would otherwise cannibalise itself
sell its parts to the repair shop—the wreckers,
Mrs Adelman would know just what to do,
everyday citizen magician
could stamp new keys and words,
and phrases like—"s h a r i n g e c o n o m i e s"

    tap tap
    tap
    return,
easy enough to share a bike, a washer, a car
but citizenship,
that's a tall order
that drops anchor
astern a tall ship of legitimacy—
a p o p-u p-s h o w
that never ended,
that built and builds
real and virtual walls
to keep the Other out,
while buying their wares for a quarter,

on a new and different black market
dredging seas
where lines are fluid
but for the geometry of dreams—of cartography,
desperate to quantify without quality control
stitched up south of the border
while Ruthenium 106
travels the seasonal reversal of winds
to sink death anew into dying young millennial's
in a great south land
and a "don't look" world
ever weighing the gains of glacier melt
unaware
of the climatic catastrophe it heralds.

Such a load of foreboding in the paper tonight among
the meaning of rainbows in Australian politics
and the price of saffron in India.

Mytho/Political waters

Who does Athena—the stolen child—favour
in this latest will to power?
Her aquagenie mother/sister Metisian lineage
or paternal Zeusian passions?

The dangerous partner
of the Great Acceleration
man and his nuclear arms race
produce the new science.

Rainbow Warriors
women for survival
peace fleets everywhere pleaded
took to the seas
wooden boats in gasping waters.

Mururoa burnt the seabed
and all it housed
hot property
these vaporised atolls
while
starwars
proliferated then destroyed
...not even Poseidon
would take a lease on this.

Denials and boycotts
for small peace-loving nations
their jelly-babies
finned not limbed
echoed Hiroshima
pre-figured

Chernobyl and Fukushima...

When the ketch *Genevieve*
sailed into the path
of a US nuclear sub
off Cockburn Sound in 86,
the women's crew
of innocent inheritors
from the coldest war
between once friends

were unafraid to drown—

their non-violent direct action
translated through rhetorical bias
into the fabric of an iron curtains
threat to national security

but
Tethys herself
in defiance of Zeus' wrecking ball reign
her grand-daughter Athena's displacement,
called up the lost from the underworld
...Persephone and Eurydice
and with Aura's help
nudged them from the reach of modern pirates
towed by sea lion relations
beyond the grasp of harm

to live and write the truth.

Un-Guard

I mean to push your buttons
with my gravid pause
pick at your fear with silence.

Your head miles ramble madly on
the demons between your ears draw swords
with the angels in the living room

Un-guard

Between times I slip away
        do the bended knee gig
in the cathedral
pay homage to things once baffling.

There's no shame in a Hail Mary.

She mends the tattered veil
around our psyche
doesn't she?

Back in ER they ask me to de-robe you
only to re-gown you
in starch stiff

hospital linens

before your quaking frame
is hoisted on to the gurney.
You won't relinquish your jocks
still have some pride
        yet a putrid poison stench
        seeps from your pores, your breath.

This ill-will
makes an attempt on your life.
Should I do a Jesus Christ
and wash your feet
in prayer
in tears
for your self betrayal?

In the confessional I declare myself
make amends to the work of the soul
long abandoned
punctuated by wars
survived by my own soldier's heart.

My bargaining is too late
        my redemption meaningless
hell's gate holds you hostage
        the graveyard calls you in.

Mont Blanc ice

Like Jonathon Livingston Seagull
your twirl through aero dynamics
was animated differently,
flirting with Mont Blanc
through extreme dance steps
the flourish from your opaque wings
...and ice-cold fate
in the sweeping flight
of divine influx...soaring boundless
into forever transfigured mist
      —Aaron on the wing.

17.07.15

Winded

Heart and lung borders
close the gate
on in-spiration

breath ascended
glances back at sorrow
the blood and bone between the sheets

winded

12.05.18

Smalls (Haiku)

'Love Carries Mom',
she wrote on her wall
without the possessive   (for DR and CF)

Surfeit tears
once swollen
best left to fall

Liquid sedation
immersion in sea
I could die here   and be happy about it

You alone are my holy one
take the human out of the prayer
and dissolve me

It's the ship you can't see
the wombat that looks like a badger
because wombat isn't yet   in the artist's hands

Alarm to waken
during the post-op graveyard shift
just in case I found the grace to surrender

A pocket full of posy
settled in the garden of
rosy metamorphosis

Enfolded by Glen Forrest
blue leschenaultia
lost cat in a trap

Mount Manypeaks remembers
bleaker days
of screaming whales

Micro Socialism

The smallness of ants
        collective mountain moving courage
        selfless and reverential
unswerving disciples of creation

their scurrying legs
        un-corrupted intention
        at the whiff of rain
weighed in by the wind rush

the call to work

Gleaning

Ah Ruth,

so practical
faithful
skilled

gleaning in a foreign field
to feed the core
and work the heart.

The rock and womb
in which a Divine genealogy
would flourish

because one woman changed her direction.

A refugee accepted (from Moab no less)
could there be a greater enemy
of the State

yet Bethlehem received her
in-corporated her
reaping more than just the harvest

a yield of Messianic progeny
who would glean from un-decidables
make them the pharmakon of the future...

because one woman changed her direction.

Refugee Mary

Patrology

leaves true Magdalene out.
Nazarene Holy
beloved
beyond Peter's ken,

Peter, who reverted to type
less than 24hrs after the resurrection
created a wench, laid waste to her witness.

Some rock.

She, and a handful of companions
set adrift, monks at sea
refugees without rudder or sail
a boat of unwanted sirens

wailing for a God transposed into matter,
whom history supposes is one man
and one divine

with no regard
for *other-ly* coloured stories
flesh wounds made word.

They limp across the Mediterranean squall
that already has so many sets of bones
and more to come

Odysseus could steer them
Hellenic demi-god

or Luke, physician of the sea,
the wiser of men

...yet the feminine sacred seems destined
to descend the abyss.

But behold!

her coracle surfaces on the shore near Marseilles

to undo the corruption of wisdom
styled as finite knowledge
that seduced so many

Holy Magdalene

not consumed by sea
but befriended ...

by some unseen intent
uncanny gesture—
of longevity.

Threshold

Thresholds are everything
if variegated, like a vernix sheath

between worlds that govern movement,
    life
    in the all-at-sea-ness of
    asylum seeking,
    the fight for terra firma
    and oxygen
    in the labour ward,
    in a world obsessed with
    bar-coded identity
    and retina display
    fixing it in
    as if mortals were in charge.

Border-zones

The current state of play
seems farcical to commentators
who want a better way to negotiate
the echoing tribal tension of thousands of years

    —different story when you live it—

Christians barely get a look in
    (too recent)
even less the women

    in this political play for god
—that takes a minimum toll of 5,000 skeletons p.a.
to re-carpet the Thalassal floor—

    from the collective descendants of
Abraham as if this was the only way to think,
    as if Wisdom had no say.

But what to do…how to reframe
the capillaries of history
that bleed into the people
like a river that's lost its course
broken into tributaries.

Negev time

Three times I went
from a different direction and tempo.
Every time, I didn't know
you were at my back
holding the stranger.

Visioning is ubiquitous here.
A few big names have left their fingerprints
over the destiny
of this ivory golden vastness
that bastes neophytes with spirit.

Clouds rest above
not given to rain,
Divine voyeurs
lacing a veil over Mysteries
not meant for mortal trade.

Airs

for JW

Aorangi
dreamed a big heart
into the Rimutaka Ranges
and outward,
heaped
tears aplenty
so fierce they pierced the land
into gargantuan fragments and ravines
like a loaded dice exploded—
        So that one day, air planes could fly over
with poets and dreamers on board
who'd ooh and ahh
and pen deep human thoughts
of big immortal wonders

in flight mode.

Yes Dante

The hell that is apathy endures,
the spirits do indeed *mourn their ancient pain*
dear Dante,
while matter
dresses itself up
chameleon style
to antagonize noble intention
and invest in idolatry and masks
that nurture nothing

Ode to Habitus

I found you in the library in the 300s
after a poor representative of your work
glossed over the precision of your genetic grammar.
Still whet my appetite drooling for the taste of you
my longing to belong to all that was in your agential field,
while dust gathered on my un-fingered covers
in the 800s ...
my bodily hexis
seeping out between pages holding hands with no one,
between the covers of others.

Different habits all together, you and I.

Yet, you led me in a dispositional dance
your own seductive bonded waltz,
kept me tumbling for your particularity of step,
or at least your disciplined instruction,
naming my structures making me address them,
only to un-dress them.
I welcomed a second bag of winds
to disrupt the discursive weight of anchorage
trip up your insistence on my certainty,
       to go colour in
       transnational reversals
inflections
       cross-pollinations
irreverent of lines of flight
and bordered dominion.

Breaking up was hard to do.

And now I've left you there in that field
freighted by your own corporeality
and Maussian assemblage
that codes your own tradition,
still fencing the tangible
my be-loved one,
you,
who tied me to the fixity
of what needed freedom
you who gave me the lens to grind my angle of vision

Trans-figuration was inevitable.

Once I left your bounded frame
—the territorial repertoire of my inheritance—
I dived fathoms to claim new capital
symbolic and otherwise, ascended
on ultra-wide renovated wings,
tampering with your collective practices
to become the agent of my own becoming,
grow a second skin with bigger gaps and spaces
        to leak through,
to breathe in
the rarefied air of these dizzy cirrus heights
        incorrect
non-constant
        flapping
refigured

knowing you wait like a carpetbagger
to give me up
hand me back to my primordial design.

Slovenian Poems

1. Bees

Royal Jelly

grown in fields without pesticides
sucked and gleaned from stigma
on calorific flowers

black swans keeping an eye on it all.

2. Sežana

Your poems did reach me Srečko.
Flew my Australian face to streets
where your words are painted on the footpath
by a different resistance.
Everything bears your name here,
your face,
Don't you know!

Filtering

Heaven rains its wisdom upon us
    —to catch the occasional drip
join it up with other beads of divine wet
to pool into a wave or a fall
capable of cleansing,
    nourishing
        or simple frolic... the *divine milieu* at play

Skin

A lifetime of work in these gloves
        of loves labour
hands held and un held...
        lines wrinkled and marked, rubbed out
        yet carrying the weight of transition
        the scars of mortality.

Fire

Inert without oxygen
ravenous with it,
I lose my breath
in fear of your swarm
       and charcoal stain.

Fish

She watches
with five-year-old awe and
reverence
the arc of the reel over
water
singing the fish to him,
        her widowed father

Brief-cased girl

She's a brief-cased girl.
Pockets
pouches and crevasses
mark the body of her text,
soft fawny exterior
slightly stained
veined and wrinkled
with a darker, warm velvet interior
a little torn and worn from rough
peak-hour handling feeling for the right bits
held together with a secret zip
and a click
clack lock.

Who am I?

I'm looking for my soul.
It was here yesterday, I know...
I was with it
but today it eludes me

like some distant star

I can't remember how to wish upon.

The 7th Wave

Greek Oceanid Metis
knows we *re* lapse to
her sea yearn for soft
motion
        the calm before the storm of birth
from her channel
then
with sinews broken
        rock the cradle
tender infant to-and-fro-ing
replicate the movement of
the chasms of deliverance
and later
as the wet fire of sex
a desperate gushing plea
gnashing liquidity

the paradoxical urge and recoil of the sea
making love to the shore and itself
and the play things
that dangle in its seduction
urgent and rushed
graceful and measured
        by the perfection of the 7th wave

Threes

I.
eternal guardianship
difficult to surrender
        a mother's polymorphous love

II.
haunting fog
and frozen dew
        the skeletal remains of winter

III.
after the swoop
of littering tourists
        the guardians of the medina clean up

The breath of trees

Everything whimpered in
    the after-glow,
    mourning carried by
    birdsong
    in the now spacious air,
    the planetary pneuma,
    transforming nature's
    smouldering
    love-objects
    into melancholy

    Fledglings un-
    nested
    by the roast,
    witness their
    companion species—
    those suffocated saplings—
    fight to give air into life
    because it is the
    work of their Being
    however maimed
    and ashed
    their kin become.

Friday night in Freo (circa 1985)

It always rains on Friday night in Freo
yet the crowd at the new Pappa's seems to thrive—
peaceniks sporting home made rainbow t shirts
sipping granitas, sucking on rollies
planning the next Action
to drive the US nukes out of the harbour
while the socialists recruit the lost and naïve
concocting Cold War propaganda
as deftly as the Russians and the Yanks,
invisible to the orange people,
and dykes on bikes
who ride on by
and play chicken with the 520 bus,
till they pull up at Gino's
and compete with French Kiss and the Bond Corporation
to order macchiato.

It's safer at the Fly by Night Club
where Kavisha lets it rip
with her angelic brand of harmonic convergence
(long before the eastern states would know her),
or if you're lucky the Dugites,
or some out of towners
if you survive the trawl in the rain
and bypass misadventure
in the pot-holed lanes
beside the markets.
—If you trip—
the food kitty won't get spent on food tonight
and you'll forget the rain till morning
while someone else watches the clock.

Disciple

If I tell you
              if I dis close
this dis closure
              what else might fall from my mouth?
Would you throw your book at
my keen head
   crucify my infantility
from the pedestal
of your intellectual eminence
... me, your exuberant junior
and stand-in?

How might you censure this precocious sage-in-waiting
       for being too enthusiastic
about the difference
       between transcendence and transubstantiation?

Would you cloak my mouth
   with your ample lips
... interrupt my stuttered discourse?

        ... in the moist folds of my inferior dreams!

All that wells
       in our meetings
              is your rage   my tears

that could distil us both.

It's transference gone pear-shaped
awash with sticky bits of angst,

and so I
> drop
by droplet
> drop
dis integrate on landing
only to re-construct my somatic and psychic architecture
> from this *corps morcelé*

for the next consumptive act of this monstrous play.

Pre-Iconic capital

for KEH

While scavenging tinder and firewood
round the ankles of Mt Ainslie—
        wheelbarrow and axe at the ready
        to find fuel for his mother's stove
        the War Memorial just taking shape—
his dog, Fido,
        chasing chips flying from the axe's slice,
landed mid-swing
beneath the young bloke's blade.
Abandoned the wood
        to his mother's misery,
nursed the dog in the shed for three days
        sticking its head back together
with love and tears and
pre-pubescent spit.
Vets were for horses in '42.

Later, in '63
as a husband and father...
who defected south of the river
from the gutters of Ainslie,
        he asked a mate in the NCDC
to put a lake at the end of his street
so he could teach his kids to swim,
        the EK Holden
not up to the Manuka Pool trek
for twice daily relief
from 105 in the shade.

Towards century's end—
a mid-lifer—
>	he marvelled at the Tower
and objected
to the building of rowing sheds
at his end of Novar Street.
Colourbond, aesthetically way out of line,
>	to the labouring brickies of the old guard.
But new wave Yarralumlans welcomed boats
and other markers.
>	Years later his granddaughter
would row from the shore
of that familial bay
>	head of a different
>	twenty-first century river.

In '13
at settler Centenary celebrations
he hears one daughter tell a story on 666 fm
of being his most wayward child
>	the Cold War
bending her politics out of shape
at Tilly's and other dangerous places.
And at a Centenary concert
on the lawns of Old Parliament House
(memorial of an-other kind)
>	he is *smoked* and Welcomed to Country
for the first time in his 81 years
>	—then sheds a tear
as a young composer
dedicates his latest Mandolin mastery
to the memory of this bloke's oldest—
her too-young
ghosted bones
hovering over
a different
Capital

Lamentacious

(Ungracious lament in a lost key)

There is no grace
in the lament
of the poet's grief...

    the archetypal
    tortured soul
    reeks of pernicious loss

eating away
with parasitic intention
the once animated life

    roaring on the pages
    of under read books
    because emoji chatter is easier

while there shedding dust
from the winds of indifference
bleeds the heart of the poet's page

    as if Keats himself were there
    between the wooded shelves
    honouring the unfathomable

grief of living through a death
dying through a living
that eclipses the soul

    renders the remainders,
    the left-behinds
    useless in the face of

the one surety
that time stops
in every heart.

I. Repose in the key of G

That universal certainty
      fare-welling the dead
doesn't come naturally.
A private rite of passage
for the dying
leaves the living
exiled, excluded
from the soul's departure,
yet
bound by grief
      attached to a
past
      tense
from missing a moment that
will too soon be history
      memory.

II. Repose in the key of B

I wore you like a cloak the day you died
the oblique mist of your soul
shrouding me
in the memorial of my skin,
      to which you clung
like a broken-hearted infant
keening for the holy milk of a
mother's breast
a lover's heart.

I thought you'd wane in Cancer
always longing for water and home
but your mercurial passions claimed your time.

Poised in the back pew of the church
mistress of your soul
witness to your malady
yet stranger to your common story,
I bow and pray repose
as St Augustine anoints you
recommends your last blessing.

III. Repose in a major key

Paradise
      re-posed
to accommodate our cantillation
for your transposition
      your middle eights
and
heart
beats
      that leave behind
a Greek chorus murmuring
in a new and major key.

IV. Repose as a major 7th

A once lifting and lilting song
        C major 7th perhaps—
pipes and plucks harmonics
willing the crescendo...
        the last note
        of the now quickened soul

PS

The last swoop of the hawk
leaves a trail of emptiness
for the remainders
whom it once fed,
as a vulning pelican
bleeds its own breast
for its young
in the leanest of times

Afterword

Poetry is typically considered a solitary art, where individuals avoid the contaminating effects of a Bloomian 'influence',[1] and work alone, charting their own paths through "the world of private emotion".[2] This can be considered a lingering trace of John Locke's concept of language: that "words, in their primary or immediate signification, stand for nothing but the ideas in the mind of him that uses them"[3]—a concept that continues to have some traction, two centuries on.

All the same, poets frequently collaborate: less often as co-authors; very often as beta readers of each other's work, and in the give and take of images, ideas and attitudes.[4] Published works by individual poets reflects this sort of relationality: a poem typically appears in a journal or anthology under one author's name but due to the effect of juxtaposition, it reads in a loose conversation with other poems. Occasionally poets co-author work; a famous example is *Ralentir Travaux* (1930), by André Breton, Paul Eluard and René Char;[5] but only a handful of other collaborations have found their way to publication.

Similarly rare is a third mode of collaboration: joint publications of two discrete voices between one set of covers. An early example is Wordsworth and Coleridge's *Lyrical Ballads*.[6] Australian examples include Jamie Grant and Graeme Kinross-Smith's *Turn Left at Any Time With Care* (1975),

---

1 Harold Bloom (1997) *The Anxiety of Influence: A Theory of Poetry* (2nd ed) New York: Oxford UP

2 Winifred Nowottny (1962) *The Language Poets Use*, London: The Athlone Press, p.60

3 John Locke (1848) *An Essay on Human Understanding and a Treatise on the Conduct of Understanding*, Philadelphia: Kay & Troutman, p.267

4 See J Webb and P Hetherington (2016) 'Slipperiness, strange attractors, and collaborative sociability', *Axon: Creative Explorations*, Issue 10: The Poetics of Collaboration (April)

5 Translated as *Slow, Under Construction* (trans Keith Waldrop), Cambridge MA: Exact Change Press, 1990

6 William Wordsworth and Samuel Taylor Coleridge (1798) *Lyrical Ballads, with a Few Other Poems*, London: J & A Arch

and *Radar* by Kevin Brophy and Nathan Curnow (2012). Reviewers sometimes seem to struggle to identify why and how the parts fit together but, responding to *Radar*, Dan Disney reaches for "Rimbaud's cri de cœur, 'Je suis l'autre'".[7] Though we do not make such a claim about our joint publication, which braids together different poetic styles in different voices, they join in the interstices crafted by shared experiences.

---

7 Dan Disney (2013) 'Review of *Radar*', *Mascara Literary Review* 4 (June 4), http://mascarareview.com/dan-disney-reviews-radar-by-nathan-curnow-and-kevin-brophy/

Notes

Play it as it lays, p.36 from 'As It Lays', Michael Chow in interview with Alex Israel, 2012

In the Paper Tonight p. 47, refers to the Obituary for Mrs Adelman in the *New York Times*, 27 November 2017.

Refugee Mary, p. 57 Jacques Derrida (in *Dissemination*. trans. Barbara Johnson. London: Athlone Press, 1981, 71-99) analyses the place of the misplaced (read as refugee, asylum seeker, displaced person) as the 'undecideables' who have the potential to become 'the pharmakon (remedy), supplement (missing thing) or hymen i.e. violation of something to cause the fusion of the self and other.'

Filtering p. 68 from *Divine Millieu: an essay on the interior life* (Fontana Books 1957) by Pierre Teilhard de Chardin who meshes science and religion, exterior and interior life. He was threatened with excommunication from the Church if her persisted joining science and religion.

Acknowledgements

The possibilities of water, p.3, stanzas 2 and 3 previously published in *Western Humanities Review* 72.1, 2018.

Attunga Point, Lake Burley Griffin, p.22 previously published in *The Lodge on the Lake: A Design Ideas Competition*, Canberra, 2015.

Icarus Icara, p.28, stanza 1 previously published in *Western Humanities Review* 72.1, 2018.

Changing sides, p.31 previously published in *The Canberra Times: Panorama,* 22 September, 2018.

An earlier version of **Mytho-political Waters, p.47** appeared in my book *Aquamorphia: Falling for water* (Interactive Publications, Carindale, 2014).

Sežana p.65 and Winded p.52 received the Zlato Priznanje (Gold Prize) for migrant poets in Slovenia and was published in August 2020, in *Paralele 23* pp. 131-132 (Funded by The Public Fund of the Republic of Slovenia for Cultural Activities Slovenian & JSKD).

Brief-cased Girl p. 70 appeared in *Meniscus* 2015, Volume 3, No. 2 p. 19

About the authors

Jen Webb is a writer and cultural theorist, and Dean of Graduate Research at the University of Canberra. She writes poetry, researches creative practive and makes and exhibits artists' books. Her most recent books are *Watching the World* (Blemish Books, 2015), *Researching Creative Writing* (Frontinus 2015), *Art and Human Rights: Contemporary Asian Contexts* (Manchester University Press 2016), and *Moving Targets* (Recent Work Press, 2018).

Shé Hawke is a poet and inter-disciplinary scholar who acknowledges the people of Ngunnawal Country on whose land most of the book was written. Her poetic, academic and personal interests centre around environmental and social justice. She is currently the Head of the Mediterranean Institute for Environmental Studies at the Science and Research Centre, Koper, Slovenia, and at the time of writing was homesick for Australian eucalypts. The book is dedicated to late loved ones Keith, Jasper, Jon, Aaron and Genevieve.

www.ingramcontent.com/pod-product-compliance
Lightning Source LLC
Chambersburg PA
CBHW020328010526
44107CB00054B/2023